D1307855

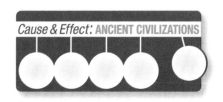

Cause & Effect:
The Ancient Maya

Other titles in the *Cause & Effect:
Ancient Civilazations* series include:

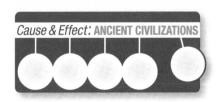

Cause & Effect: ANCIENT CIVILIZATIONS

Cause & Effect: The Ancient Maya

Stephen Currie

ReferencePoint Press®

San Diego, CA

© 2018 ReferencePoint Press, Inc.
Printed in the United States

For more information, contact:
ReferencePoint Press, Inc.
PO Box 27779
San Diego, CA 92198
www.ReferencePointPress.com

LIBRARY OF CONGRESS CATALOGING-IN-PUBLICATION DATA

Names: Currie, Stephen, 1960– author.
Title: Cause & Effect: The Ancient Maya/by Stephen Currie.
Other titles: Ancient Maya
Description: San Diego, CA: ReferencePoint Press, 2017. | Series: Cause & Effect: Ancient Civilizations | Includes bibliographical references and index. | Audience: Grade 9-12.
Identifiers: LCCN 2017017404 (print) | LCCN 2017018647 (ebook) | ISBN 9781682821572 (eBook) | ISBN 9781682821565 (hardback)
Subjects: LCSH: Mayas.
Classification: LCC F1435 (ebook) | LCC F1435 .C87 2017 (print) | DDC 972.81/016--dc23
LC record available at https://lccn.loc.gov/2017017404

CONTENTS

"History is a complex study of the many causes that have influenced happenings of the past and the complicated effects of those varied causes."

—William & Mary School of Education,
Center for Gifted Education

U nderstanding the causes and effects of historical events and time periods is rarely simple. The largest and most influential empire of ancient India, for instance, came into existence largely because of a series of events set in motion by Persian and Greek invaders. Although the Mauryan Empire was both wealthy and well organized and benefited enormously from strong rulers and administrators, the disarray sowed by invading forces created an opening for one of India's most ambitious and successful ancient rulers—Chandragupta, the man who later came to be known in the West as the "Indian Julius Caesar." Had conditions in India at the time been different, the outcome might have been something else altogether.

The value of analyzing cause and effect in the context of ancient civilizations, therefore, is not necessarily to identify a single cause for a singular event. The real value lies in gaining a greater understanding of that civilization as a whole and being able to recognize the many factors that gave shape and direction to its rise, its development, its fall, and its lasting importance. As outlined by the National Center for History in the Schools at the University of California–Los Angeles, these factors include "the importance of the individual in history . . . the influence of ideas, human interests, and beliefs; and . . . the role of chance, the accidental and the irrational."

ReferencePoint's Cause & Effect: Ancient Civilizations series examines some of the world's most interesting and important civilizations by focusing on various causes and consequences. For instance, in *Cause & Effect: Ancient India*, a chapter explores how one Indian ruler helped transform Buddhism into a world religion. And in *Cause & Effect: Ancient Egypt*, one chapter delves into the importance of the Nile River in the development of Egyptian civilization. Every book in the series includes thoughtful discussion of questions like these—supported by facts, examples, and a mix of fully documented primary and secondary source quotes. Each title also includes an overview of the civilization so that readers have a broad context for understanding the more detailed discussions of causes and their effects.

The value of such study is not limited to the classroom; it can also be applied to many areas of contemporary life. The ability to analyze and interpret history's causes and consequences is a form of critical thinking. Critical thinking is crucial in many professions, ranging from law enforcement to science. Critical thinking is also essential for developing an educated citizenry that fully understands the rights and obligations of living in a free society. The ability to sift through and analyze complex processes and events and identify their possible outcomes enables people in that society to make important decisions.

The Cause & Effect: Ancient Civilizations series has two primary goals. One is to help students think more critically about the human societies that once populated our world and develop a true understanding of their complexities. The other is to help build a foundation for those students to become fully participating members of the society in which they live.

IMPORTANT EVENTS IN THE HISTORY OF THE ANCIENT MAYA

260
A volcanic eruption in the Maya highlands disrupts trade and displaces populations.

BCE 2600
Maya civilization is generally considered to have begun.

BCE 200
The first Maya stelae are created.

484
The rulers of Caracol build a network of raised causeways to make travel easier.

BCE 1000 / CE 300   400   500

BCE 700
The Maya develop a system of writing.

CE 250
The Maya classic period begins.

435
The dynasty of Yax K'uk Mo' begins in Copan, encompassing fifteen rulers in all.

500
Tikal becomes the first great city of the Maya.

562
Calakmul becomes the most powerful city in the Maya territory.

615
K'inich Janaab' Pakal I begins a sixty-eight-year reign over the city of Palenque.

1492
Christopher Columbus makes his first voyage to the Americas.

692
Three large temples are dedicated at Palenque.

900
The classic period of Maya history ends.

1562
Diego de Landa destroys most of the surviving Maya codices.

600　　900　　1200　　1500

600
Tikal's population reaches about half a million people.

869
The last stela is completed in Tikal.

1517
The Spanish reach the Yucatán Peninsula.

790
A large mural is completed at the city of Bonampak.

The Maya World

Historians and archaeologists often struggle to answer all the questions they have about civilizations dating from many centuries ago. The ancient Egyptians, the Babylonians, the Inca of South America, the Mali Empire of West Africa: These and many other great cultures of the past are not as well understood today as researchers would like. Evidence is often simply lacking to answer questions even about basic facts such as a society's population, the geographic extent of a culture's influence, or the years during which the culture was at its peak.

In some cases scholars know the important events of a civilization's history but not necessarily the exact order of these events. In other cases it may not be entirely clear whether people referred to in ancient texts were real, mythical, or some combination of the two. And the connections between different events or aspects of many civilizations have been entirely lost over the years. Cause and effect, in particular, can be difficult to unravel. At a remove of many centuries, especially when documentary evidence is scarce, it may be impossible to identify just why the leaders of a particular culture made the decisions they did, for example, or what caused a particular religion to grow in popularity while another did not.

These issues are perhaps particularly significant in the case of the Maya, a Central American people whose civilization flourished through nearly all of the first millennium CE. Although the descendants of the Maya still carry on parts of the culture, most of what scholars know about the so-called classic period of Maya culture (roughly 250–900 CE) has been painstakingly reconstructed from artifacts the early Maya left behind. These include the ruins of great cities, many of them nearly swallowed by rain forest overgrowth in the centuries since they were abandoned. They also include sculptures and occasional paintings, a variety of tools, a handful of books, a number of monuments—many of them with inscriptions—and an elaborate calendar.

These and other artifacts have been invaluable for scholars who are eager to learn about the Maya. Through detailed study of materials remaining from the classic period, archaeologists and historians have

10

successfully solved any number of puzzles about Maya life. Over time experts learned how to read the Maya system of writing, for example. They have also identified the names and responsibilities of dozens of major gods and goddesses, determined some of the most important trade routes used by the Maya, and arrived at reasonable estimates of the number of people who lived in the various urban centers. They have even deciphered the Maya calendar, which relies on an astonishingly complex series of cycles and counts to identify days and years.

Many Questions Remain

Still, much about the world of the Maya remains a question mark. Part of the reason is that many artifacts from the classic period no longer exist. Plenty of objects have disappeared in the hundreds of years since the Maya civilization was at its height. Tools have been repurposed, paintings have faded, and jewels and sculptures have been taken from ruined buildings by looters and thieves. Moreover, objects made from plaster, wood, and similar materials are prone to deterioration in the hot, humid Central American rain forest. Thus, very few wooden carvings, murals, or structures crafted from wood have survived to the present day. These gaps in the historical record have created gaps in modern understanding of the Maya as well.

To make matters worse, the Spanish who conquered much of the Maya homelands in the 1500s ordered the destruction of many ancient objects sacred to the Maya. The Spaniards were generally focused on Christianizing the descendants of the Maya and believed that the remnants of a non-Christian civilization would interfere with that goal. In particular, the Europeans set out to destroy Maya codices, or folding books, most of which dated from centuries earlier. "We found a great number of books," Spanish monk Diego de Landa reported in a book he wrote about the Maya. In that book, published in 1566, he noted, "As they contained nothing in which there was not to be seen superstition and lies of the devil, we burned them all."[1] The information and ideas within

"We found a great number of books. As they contained nothing in which there was not to be seen superstition and lies of the devil, we burned them all."[1]

—Spanish monk Diego de Landa in 1566

A painting depicts ancient Maya performing a ceremony at a temple. The Maya civilization flourished during most of the first millennium CE.

the burned codices would have been extremely informative to modern researchers; unfortunately, no one will ever know what they contained.

Nor do scholars always agree about how to interpret the available evidence. Very often existing information about the Maya is scanty or ambiguous; it could be understood in either of two ways, if not more. No one knows, for instance, whether Maya farmland was owned by individual people, by family groups, or by the state; the evidence is unclear. Similarly, there is much controversy about the reasons for the sudden end of the classic period around 900. The origins of ball games, the years in which battles took place, the amount of power actually wielded by the people who held the throne: Different scholars, examining similar pieces of evidence, have sometimes come to very different conclusions.

In the end, although scholars over the years have done a remarkable job exploring the details of the Maya world, much about the Maya remains a mystery. Ambiguous evidence and missing artifacts together create more question marks than researchers would like. Perhaps someday new evidence will be revealed that will answer some of the dozens of questions that remain about Maya life. Or perhaps experts will discover new ways of looking at existing evidence to help resolve some of the conflicts that persist today.

In the meantime, scholars and interested observers alike must live with uncertainty about certain details of Maya culture. "Who were these people that built this city?"[2] wondered John Lloyd Stephens, an American explorer who was among the first to study the Maya, upon finding the ruins of the city Copan in 1839. Thanks to research carried out by Stephens and many others, experts are much better equipped to answer this question than they once were. But no one will ever resolve all the uncertainties about the Maya and their world.

CHAPTER ONE

A Brief History of the Ancient Maya

The Maya civilization was located in Central America, specifically the Yucatán Peninsula of what is now Mexico and the adjoining regions of modern-day Belize and Guatemala. Most of this area is low lying, though part of the region is mountainous, and much of it is hot, humid, and wet. Daytime temperatures across the area frequently reach 95°F (35°C), and rainfall in some places can amount to as much as 100 inches (254 cm). In this climate plants grow quickly, with trees able to reach enormous dimensions. "Gigantic trees predominate,"[3] writes anthropologist T. Patrick Culbert, noting that the tallest trees routinely reach more than 100 feet (30 m) above the forest floor. Indeed, much of the southern part of Maya territory qualifies as a tropical or subtropical rain forest.

Determining where the Maya culture flourished is easy, but identifying *when* Maya civilization was in existence is a much more difficult question. Some scholars argue that the beginnings of Maya culture can be seen in the arts, economy, and social structure of Central Americans living as far back as 2500 BCE, and nearly all experts agree that an identifiable Maya culture was starting to emerge in the area by 1000 BCE or so. Over the next millennium—and beyond—the culture continued to grow both economically and politically. At the same time, the social structure gradually grew more and more sophisticated. By about 250 CE, researchers generally agree, Maya civilization had reached a high point. In art, science, warfare, government, and many other areas, the Maya had arrived at a position of dominance over the peoples who lived elsewhere in the region. The Maya had become one of the great civilizations of the time.

After reaching this peak, moreover, Maya civilization remained at this powerful level for many centuries. Today the years from about 250 to around 900 are generally known as the classic period of Maya civilization; when modern people discuss the Maya, they usually are referring to these years. During this time the Maya hold on the Yucatán and surrounding areas was never in dispute, and the culture's influence stretched far beyond its territorial borders. While it can be difficult to compare one civilization to another, the evidence seems clear that no society anywhere in the Americas reached a similar level of prosperity, knowledge of the world, and political power during the Maya classic period, and few from any other era could rival it until the coming of the Europeans. "In many ways," concludes archaeologist John S. Henderson, "Maya culture is the most complex ever to arise in the New World."[4]

> "In many ways, Maya culture is the most complex ever to arise in the New World."[4]
>
> —Archaeologist John S. Henderson

The classic period did not last forever, however. Sometime around 900 CE, Maya society underwent massive dislocations. For reasons that are not completely understood, the civilization abruptly entered a period of decline. It continued on a less dominant level for several centuries; many aspects of the classic period remained part of daily life among the people of the region, but the political and economic strength of the classic period was gone, as were the remarkable art and architecture of the earlier years. Much later, the arrival of the Spanish in the early 1500s permanently changed Central American politics, government, and customs and destroyed a great deal of what remained of Maya culture and Maya ways.

Nonetheless, as a people the Maya are not extinct. Today the descendants of the Maya still live in the rain forests and highlands of the Yucatán and adjoining areas. Their languages, their cultures, and their relationship to the land around them bear many resemblances to their ancestors of the classic period; but their power and their wealth do not compare with their counterparts from a previous millennium. "Millions of people still grow up speaking Maya languages as their first tongues," points out Henderson, "and wrest a living from the land principally by means of the ancient traditional methods. . . . In some regions the old gods still command primary allegiance, and everywhere Christianity is tempered with a strong . . . [combination] of native beliefs and practices."[5] Though the great Maya civilization no longer holds sway in Central America, the descendants of the Maya still make their mark on the world.

The World of the Ancient Maya

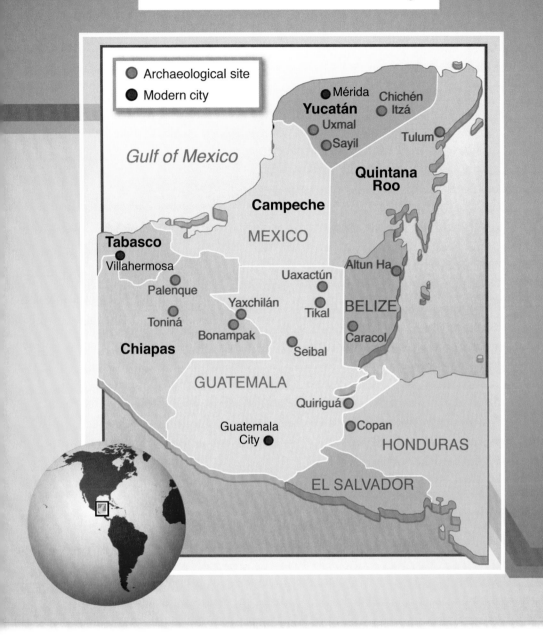

Political and Social Structure

Maya culture, especially of the classic period, had several important hallmarks. One was a relatively loose political structure. Unlike the two other great American civilizations that followed the Maya—the Aztec of the area around Mexico City and the Inca in South

America—the Maya did not have a strong central government. Instead, their territory was divided into many smaller political units that functioned more or less independently. These units shared important cultural features: The people of one political subdivision typically worshipped the same gods, ate the same foods, and used the same construction techniques as others who lived nearby. But there was no single emperor of the Maya world. Researchers Linda Schele and David Freidel liken the Maya political landscape to the dozens of duchies and principalities that characterized feudal Europe or to the city-states of ancient Greece. As they put it, the Maya world consisted of "little countries that were politically autonomous, yet culturally, socially, and economically interdependent."[6]

Each political unit was governed by a royal family that featured kings, queens, lords, and various other nobles. For the most part power was handed down from fathers to sons and occasionally to daughters, though it could also travel to brothers, uncles, or nephews. In the Maya worldview, these aristocrats—especially those who wielded great power—ranked somewhere above ordinary people. At the very least, they served as intermediaries between gods and human beings, and there is evidence that some of the Maya leaders were perceived to be minor divinities themselves. Certainly Maya monarchs were expected to be at the center of a variety of religious rituals, including bloodletting—the practice of piercing their bodies, including tongues and ears, with thorns or other sharp objects and then dedicating the resulting blood as an offering to the gods.

Not all nobles served as government leaders. Others held positions as priests, scribes, astronomers, government bureaucrats, or military officers—each a position requiring education and good breeding, and each demanding respect from the lower orders of society. Though the nobility made up only a small share of the Maya population—by some estimates, scarcely more than about 2 percent of the total—members of the aristocracy played an enormous role in Maya life. In addition to dominating Maya society politically, aristocrats controlled most of the culture's wealth as well. Indeed, nobles could easily be identified by their fine clothing and jewelry, the size and style of their homes, and even what they ate and drank. Chocolate, for example, was a great delicacy among the Maya. But only the richest could afford to drink a cup of chocolate every day.

Monarchs, priests, and other nobles made up the Maya upper class. Below them was a middle class consisting of merchants, architects, and minor government functionaries as well as artisans: craftspeople who were responsible for making tools, ceramics, jewelry, and other goods for decorative purposes as well as ordinary household use. Members of the middle class were respected within Maya society, though they lacked the economic and political power of the aristocracy. Even though they outnumbered the members of the nobility, the middle class still made up only a small part of Maya society: Most scholars agree that they accounted for less than 10 percent of all Maya.

The great bulk of Maya belonged to the lower classes. Most of these were poor farmers, tied to the land, who labored long hours to raise food for themselves—and for the upper and middle classes, whose responsibilities did not permit them the time to grow their own food. Others were servants for the nobility. Still others worked as unskilled laborers in urban areas, helping construct palaces, temples, and the open-air plazas that were frequent features of Maya architecture. The homes of the commoners tended to be made of bark and thatch, materials that rotted quickly in the humid Central American climate, and the remaining written records of the classic period focus heavily on the upper classes. As a result, not much historical or archaeological evidence remains to give a clear indication of what life was like for the poorest Maya.

Cities, Farms, and Commerce

Like the ancient Greeks and Romans, the Maya were capable and enthusiastic constructors of cities. The biggest urban areas, such as Tikal in present-day Guatemala and Caracol in what is now Belize, had populations that probably exceeded one hundred thousand at their peak. The Maya have become justly celebrated for their urban architecture. Maya designers and laborers constructed enormous buildings from stone, including temples, palaces, and public plazas that were often connected by causeways, stone streets, and staircases. The interiors of the buildings were often cramped

"The impact of a reconstructed Maya building in the tropical sunlight is breathtaking."[7]

—Anthropologist T. Patrick Culbert

The ruins of the Maya city of Tikal (shown) are today an archaeological site. The Maya are known for their stunning urban architecture.

and dark—the Maya tended to build thick walls to support the heavy roofs featured on most large structures—but the exteriors were especially impressive. "Angles and overhangs, inset corners and projecting moldings—a whole series of tricks were used to play with light and shadow," notes Culbert. "The impact of a reconstructed Maya building in the tropical sunlight is breathtaking."[7]

It is not necessary for travelers to visit a reconstructed building to see the effectiveness of Maya architectural techniques. Though virtually all of these buildings were shrouded in overgrowth when explorers and archaeologists came upon them in the nineteenth and early twentieth centuries, these visitors had no difficulty imagining what the

Maya Mythology

One important aspect of the Maya religion involves the culture's complex mythology. Long after the classic period, many of the Maya myths were recorded in a book known as the Popul Vuh. These legends describe events such as the creation of the earth, several unsuccessful attempts on the part of the gods to make human beings, and the exploits of the Hero Twins, two brothers who were instrumental in defeating several evil gods early in the history of the world.

Maya mythology is known for its stark and often unsettling images. These include, for example, a ball filled with sharp blades designed to kill an opponent, a skull that impregnates a young woman by spitting on her palm, and a severed head being used as a ball in a game. In one story, one of the Hero Twins cuts the other to pieces and then miraculously brings him back to life as the evil gods look on. When two of the gods demand that the same be done to them, the brothers happily hack them apart—but then do not resurrect them. Despite, or perhaps because of, the violence of these and other stories, Maya myths are frequently retold by writers and story-tellers today.

constructions had looked like in their heyday. The cities were clearly "works of art," concluded John Lloyd Stephens, who visited the Maya homelands in the mid-1800s. "Nothing ever impressed me more forcibly than the spectacle of this once great and lovely city,"[8] Stephens added, referring to Palenque, once a thriving metropolis in the western part of Maya territory. Stephens's impressions are echoed time and again in the writings of other travelers as well.

Beyond the city limits, the landscape included many fewer large buildings and many more farms. The Maya relied heavily on agriculture to produce the food they needed. There were few herding animals in the Americas, virtually none of them native to the Maya's Central American territories; and while the rain forests were home to some game animals, the Maya homeland did not have the abundance of bison, deer, and wild boars found in other parts of the continent. Instead, the Maya grew crops, most notably corn, beans, and squash.

They made heavy use of the slash-and-burn agricultural technique, common in other parts of the world as well, in which they cut down trees and bushes and then set a controlled fire to produce a smooth field suitable for farming. This method allowed them to turn a section of forest into a farm relatively quickly—important as the population increased.

To ensure sufficient food for everyone, the Maya developed transportation systems capable of moving harvested crops from the relatively unpopulated countryside to the high-density cities—and did so without engines, pack animals, or carts with wheels. Primarily they used canoes and other boats to travel up and down the region's rivers. When overland travel was necessary, they strapped goods to the backs of lower-status men who acted as porters, among them slaves who had originally been captured in battle. These same transportation systems were also used to move trade goods such as food, precious and semiprecious stones, salt, tools, and decorative feathers. During the classic period in particular, commerce boosted the wealth and standard of living of people and leaders throughout the Maya homelands—sometimes dramatically.

Knowledge, Art, and Religion

In addition to being enthusiastic traders, creative architects, and able farmers, the Maya are noted today for several other skills and abilities. Primary among these is the Maya interest in science and learning. The Maya calendar, derived from thousands upon thousands of hours of observation of the heavens, was quite sophisticated—and accurate—for its time. Not until the Renaissance centuries afterward did Europe produce a calendar that could match the one used by the Maya. The Maya number system, which relied on place value and was based on multiples of twenty and five, was far easier to use for calculation than the systems used by the ancient Egyptians, Babylonians, or Romans, for example. And the Maya developed a complex writing system that made use of glyphs, elaborate symbols that could stand for sounds, word parts, or entire words. Though the descendants of the Maya lost the ability to read these glyphs long ago, modern scholars have been able to reconstruct the meanings of many writings that survive.

Art, too, was a focus of Maya culture. Maya artists frequently painted elaborate murals on the inner and outer walls of buildings. Many of these have faded with time and have been lost to history. Those that survive often depict scenes of upper-class life; one example, unearthed in 2010, shows a king and his entourage. Others focus on stories from Maya mythology. The Maya were also highly skilled stoneworkers, using limestone and other materials to create sculptures and carvings. The focus for most artists was on developing a naturalistic style showing subjects as they truly were. As museum curator James Doyle puts it, "Sculptors showed realistic portraits of divine lords, courtly ladies, captives, and deities."[9] The permanence of stone means that many Maya sculptures and carvings, old as they are, can still be found in museums in Central America and elsewhere.

The Maya's interest in stonework extended to jewelry as well. The upper classes, in particular, often wore necklaces, bracelets, and beads. Jewelry could be made from a variety of different materials, but the most coveted designs were made from jade. A greenish stone found in only a few parts of the Maya homelands, jade was thought to be exceptionally beautiful. It also symbolized several important concepts to the Maya, among them water and new growth, and was sought after for this reason as well. Although jade was popular, its use was limited largely to the nobility; it was simply too expensive for even the middle class to afford. Not only was jade difficult to find, which put its cost out of reach of all but the very rich, but working with it was slow and time consuming. "A single small jade carving must have taken a craftsman several months to complete,"[10] note Schele and Freidel.

Among the Maya, jewelry and art were important because of their beauty, and scientific knowledge was sometimes valued for its own sake. But art objects and scientific information also held religious significance. Carvings and beads played important roles in rituals designed to help the Maya communicate with the gods, and the elaborate Maya calendar was used in part to assist priests in determining the most propitious time to carry out religious rites. That made sense, for religion permeated

"A single small jade carving must have taken a craftsman several months to complete."[10]

—Scholars and authors Linda Schele and David Freidel

The Maya are known for their works of stone, from great public plazas to personal adornments. They greatly prized jewelry made of jade, such as that shown here.

all aspects of Maya life. The Maya worshipped dozens of gods, in addition to the quasi-divine status they afforded the most powerful rulers; and they were certain that these deities were deeply involved in the lives of people on earth. Accordingly, they offered sacrifices—including human sacrifice, usually of prisoners of war—that were designed to make

During the twentieth century a scholar named J. Eric S. Thompson argued that the Maya were a fundamentally peaceful people. Thompson based this claim primarily on the fact that no archaeologist had yet identified defensive structures around Maya cities. He concluded that warfare was uncommon and postulated that Maya society was governed by generally nonviolent priests. Thompson's views were influential among other experts and in the popular imagination. Indeed, many books from the mid-twentieth century state that the Maya seldom engaged in violence.

Today, however, researchers no longer accept Thompson's argument. New information has made it clear that the Maya were considerably more violent than Thompson and his followers believed. In fact, every Maya monarch had his or her share of well-equipped and well-respected soldiers, and battles between competing city-states were common. Though defensive walls are difficult to find using archaeological techniques, they were certainly present at large cities such as Tikal and Aguateca. Finally, experts are now aware that Maya religious rites made liberal use of the shedding of blood, with the tongues, lips, and flesh of nobles being pierced to draw blood as an offering to the gods, and human sacrifice was practiced as well. Today the evidence is clear: The Maya were many things, but peaceful was not among them.

the gods look more favorably upon them. The Maya also built impressive temples, many of them in the shape of a pyramid, in hopes of pleasing the gods.

The Maya were a complex people who constructed an equally complex society. From commerce to religion, from mathematics to architecture, Maya civilization was innovative and distinctive. Politically and economically dominant in their part of the Americas, the Maya maintained their power and influence for a remarkably long period of time. The six or seven centuries during which the classic period flourished is more than twice as long as the entire life span of the United States. It is no wonder that the Maya continue to attract attention today from scholars, students, and ordinary people alike.

CHAPTER TWO

How Did Geography Help Shape Maya Civilization?

Focus Questions

1. Which of these played the greatest role in shaping Maya civilization: vegetation, climate, or soil? Explain your answer.
2. In what ways was terrace agriculture an improvement over slash-and-burn techniques—and why?
3. What trade goods might have been particularly desirable in inland areas of the Maya homeland—and why?

Geographic factors can have an enormous effect on cultures and societies. The typical clothing worn by the people of a given culture, for example, is often based on the type of weather that prevails where they live: People in the tropics wear few clothes, and people in subarctic regions wear many. Similarly, large-scale agriculture is easier to develop in flat temperate zones where rainfall is common than in mountainous deserts. Even empire building can be influenced by geographical considerations. "England and France and Spain and Portugal founded worldwide colonial empires, but Switzerland and Poland and Greece did not," points out anthropologist Jared Diamond. "The former countries did, and the latter countries did not, have Atlantic Ocean ports."[11]

It should come as no surprise that much of Maya culture was influenced by the topography, climate, and natural resources of the Yucatán and the surrounding areas in which the Maya made their homes. The Maya created a distinctive society with features—trade, architecture, agriculture, art—that were based, at least in part, on the geographic realities of their region. The geographic factors, indeed, helped determine how the Maya lived and served to push Maya society in certain directions. The land, the weather, and the topography of the Maya homeland helped make Maya civilization all that it was.

Environment and Landscape

The Maya lived—and flourished—in a diverse landscape. As archaeologist Robert J. Sharer writes, "For its size, the Maya area represents one of the most varied environments on earth."[12] The largest section of the Maya homeland consisted of tropical or subtropical rain forest, sometimes called the Maya Tropical Forest today. The climate of this region is marked by high temperatures, high rainfall, and higher humidity. In much of the region today—conditions were likely similar during the Maya classic period—average summer temperatures hover above 90°F (32°C). Winters are cooler, but even in January the temperature rarely dips much below 70°F (21°C). Rain is frequent, too, especially in the summer months.

> "For its size, the Maya area represents one of the most varied environments on earth."[12]
>
> —Archaeologist Robert J. Sharer

The Central American rain forest is noted not just for hot, wet weather, but for biodiversity as well. The region is home to an extensive array of plant and animal species, some of them found in few other parts of the globe. "All told," writes anthropologist James D. Nations, "the Maya Tropical Forest is home to more than 3,400 species of vascular plants [land plants such as bushes, flowers, and trees], 60 species of freshwater fish, 42 of amphibians, 121 of reptiles, at least 571 of birds, and 163 of mammals."[13] Notable animals of the Central American rain forest include jaguars, crocodiles, butterflies, and several species of monkey; common plants include tulip trees, palms, and a variety of brightly colored flowers. The plants of the Maya region, moreover, are not only numerous but quick to grow. It is likely that the Maya had to engage in intensive efforts to prune back bushes, vines, and trees to keep the forest from encroaching on cities, farms, and villages.

Rain forest is the dominant habitat in the Maya homeland, but Maya territory also included highlands—plains and occasional mountains situated at higher altitudes overlooking the low-elevation rain forests. These highlands are located far enough above sea level—and

The region where the Maya lived is one of the most environmentally and biologically diverse on the planet. The jaguar (shown) is just one of many creatures that call this area home.

far enough north of the equator—to give them a noticeably different climate from the rain forests below. Temperatures are lower, especially in the winter, and rainfall, though still high by the standards of many other parts of the world, is not nearly as high as in the rain forest. In addition, the tree cover in the highlands is less dense, wildlife is less varied, and vegetation grows more slowly.

The rain forest and the highlands represented the geographic extremes of Maya territory, but the region also included a variety of smaller geographic zones, all with their own defining characteristics. Some of the Maya lived along the coastlines of the Atlantic or Pacific Oceans, for instance, while others lived inland, in areas notable for tall limestone cliffs. Some parts of Maya territory had easy access to freshwater in the form of lakes, rivers, and subterranean caverns that could serve as natural wells; others had freshwater only when it rained. Though the greatest share of Maya territory consisted of humid subtropical rain forests, significant portions of the region were very different.

The varying types of landforms and climates in the region occupied by the Maya played important roles in shaping Maya culture and civilization. The massive palaces and temples constructed by the Maya, for instance, were largely made from limestone. Limestone was sturdy and easy to work with, and it seems likely that Maya leaders found it appealing from an aesthetic point of view; but more important, Maya builders used limestone because it was plentiful in certain parts of the Maya territory. Similarly, Maya books did not use paper or papyrus. Rather, they used a thicker, more durable material called *huun*, which Diego de Landa described as "made from the roots of a tree."[14] In the humid climate of the rain forest, European-style paper would have disintegrated quickly. The Maya developed the stronger, more cloth-like *huun* to ensure that their records would last. The use of both limestone and *huun* serves as a simple example of how geography affected the way the Maya lived.

Agriculture

Nowhere was the connection between culture and geography more apparent than in food production. Some of the Maya who lived along the coastlines included fish in their diet, and nobles occasionally ate meat obtained by hunting game animals such as deer or wild pigs. But the few indigenous game or herding animals were insufficient to feed everyone. The realities of the Central American environment thus required that the Maya make heavy use of agriculture to provide food. Indeed, to support the expanding population of the late classic period, it was necessary for the Maya to grow as many crops as possible. The challenge was to find the farming techniques that were most suitable for the lands, soils, and climates of the area.

For some time archaeologists believed that Maya farmers in the rain forest used slash-and-burn techniques almost exclusively. More recent research suggests that this view is not quite accurate. Though the slash-and-burn method was certainly common, experts now agree that the Maya made use of other methods as well to raise crop yields in the poor soils of the rain forest.

These methods included, in particular, an innovative system of canals designed to drain low-lying swamps and convert these wetlands into productive agricultural territory. Farmers began by digging ditches in the marshy ground and piling the earth from the ditches onto the soil nearby. This had the effect of providing drier soil in which crops were better able to grow than in the wet swamps of the region. The soil from the ditches, moreover, was richer in nutrients than typical rain forest soils. Over time the ditches were often widened until they became more like canals, on occasion measuring dozens of feet across.

Like the slash-and-burn technique, this method was a good response to the realities of life in areas not blessed with naturally productive soils. "This drained field agriculture," writes anthropologist Heather McKillop, "allowed year-round farming in areas that were otherwise not arable."

Heather McKillop, *The Ancient Maya: New Perspectives*. Santa Barbara, CA: ABC-CLIO, 2004, p. 127.

The geography of the Maya homeland included several regions suitable for agriculture. The best of these areas were those lying at high elevations, where soils were reasonably fertile, rainfall was plentiful but not excessive, and the temperatures were not unrelentingly high. Accordingly, the Maya developed techniques that were especially effective in these landscapes. Probably the most common of these was terrace farming, a method that involves constructing stone walls to sculpt hillsides into small, flat fields known as terraces. Terrace farming ensures that rainfall pools on these small fields rather than washing seeds and plantings down the hills. The method improves crop yield considerably, compared to planting directly on the slopes. The process of creating the terraces could be time consuming and labor intensive, but once the walls were in place, the technique allowed farmers to raise a decent crop nearly every year.

It was fortunate for the Maya that the highlands were conducive to producing good crops, because the same could not be said for the

The Maya lived in the jungles and inland highlands, as well as coastal areas. Shown is a Maya stone structure built on cliffs overlooking the Caribbean Sea near Tulum, Mexico.

rain forest. Although native plants typically grow quickly and easily in a hot, moist environment, rain forest soils around the world are not usually well suited for agriculture, and the rain forests of Central America are no exception. In cooler and drier forest systems, such as most of the forests of the United States, the nutrients contained in dead leaves, decaying animals, and fallen trees are typically absorbed into the soil, making the earth more productive and encouraging the growth of crops. In rain forest environments, however, many of the nutrients contained in plant and animal life are broken down by insects and bacteria before they ever reach the soil. In addition, the downpours that characterize a tropical rain forest often wash minerals out of the earth and into the rivers. Without sufficient levels of minerals and nutrients, the soil cannot easily produce good crops.

Slash-and-Burn Agriculture

Still, the Maya needed to produce food even in the poor soils of the rain forest. There was simply not enough prime agricultural territory in the higher elevations to feed everyone. In an effort to increase crop yield in the lowlands, the Maya used a farming method known as slash-and-burn, or swidden, agriculture. The process, used by other peoples in similar climates elsewhere across the world, was straightforward. "Together," writes author Victoria Schlesinger, "a family cut down a section of forest, clearing it back with stone axes and fire, to open the ground for planting."[15] The flames leveled the remaining stumps and brush, with the resulting nutrient-rich ash mixing into the soil, and created a plot of cleared land where crops could be planted. Even today farmers in Guatemala and the Yucatán often use slash-and-burn techniques, with farmers using sticks to dig into the soil of a newly burned field to plant seeds and harvesting the resulting corn, beans, or other crops at the end of the growing season.

"Together, a family cut down a section of forest, clearing it back with stone axes and fire, to open the ground for planting."[15]

—Author Victoria Schlesinger

The slash-and-burn method was not ideal. For one thing, the technique required an enormous amount of time and energy. "Maya

31

The Maya developed many agricultural techniques suited to their topography. One such technique was terracing, which is still used today in some parts of the world.

farming technology required backbreaking labor and patience," notes author Lynn V. Foster. "There were no steel axes for felling trees, no oxen to plow the fields."[16] More seriously, the fields could not be used year after year. In most cases the nutritional content of the new soil could produce crops for only a single growing season. Once the crops had been harvested, the field needed to rest, or lie fallow, for a period of two or three years, sometimes more. Farmers were thus forced to abandon the field and create other plots of cleared land elsewhere. The system was inefficient, with large swaths of forest land lying idle at any given time.

But for all its problems, slash-and-burn agriculture allowed the Maya to grow food in a region with soils that would not ordinarily have been able to produce many crops. In conjunction with other techniques used in more fertile parts of the region, the slash-and-burn method gave the Maya enough food to enable them to keep their population fed—and to keep a complex and urbanized society running for hundreds of years. Had Maya civilization sprung up in a more fertile, productive region, such as the American Midwest, the Maya would not have needed to use slash-and-burn techniques. In a different environment Maya farmers would almost surely have chosen more efficient farming methods over swidden agriculture. Given the realities of the land where the Maya lived, however, the slash-and-burn method might well have been the best option available. In this way the geography of the region where the Maya lived helped shape the farming methods they used.

Geography and Commerce

A second example of the impact of geography on Maya culture involves trade. Because the landscapes and climates across the Maya homelands were not identical, certain regions were richer in some resources than others. As T. Patrick Culbert writes, the plants and animals of the rain forest provided "hardwoods for houses and furniture, boxes and trinkets, [and] fuel; resin—from the copal tree—for ceremonial incense; dazzling plumes for the costumes of the elite; jaguar pelts for clothing and . . . for the king's pillow covers."[17] Other regions of the Maya homeland either lacked these items or did not have them in abundance. But these regions had plenty of different resources instead, including fish, salt, or various types of rock, such as limestone, jade, and obsidian.

For many reasons, items such as these were valuable or necessary not just in one region of the Maya homeland but across most of Maya territory. For example, not only does salt improve the flavor of food, it is necessary for good health. That was especially true in

Maya society, because the standard corn-based diet of the Maya was naturally very low in salt. Thus, salt was in high demand throughout the region. Limestone, similarly, was required for large-scale building projects, jade was frequently used in Maya artwork, and members of the nobility sometimes wore decorative animal furs or colorful feathers to indicate their high status. Given the widespread need for these items, the obvious solution was to develop extensive trade routes throughout the region in which goods and resources abundant in one place could be easily exchanged for goods and resources abundant in another.

Indeed, trade became a hallmark of the Maya classic period. Large sailing canoes laden with trade goods traversed the rivers and even the ocean coasts of the region. Though the Maya lacked pack animals or wheeled vehicles, they carved rudimentary roads through the rain forests so that people could carry goods overland as well. In this way limestone and surplus corn moved from the highlands to the lowlands, salt traveled from the shorelines of the northern Yucatán to the inland forests, and furs and feathers were transported from areas rich in wildlife to those where animals were less abundant. Even years afterward commerce was an important part of the lives of the Maya descendants. During the 1500s Landa wrote that "the occupation to which [the Maya] had the greatest inclination was trade, carrying salt and cloth and slaves to the land of Ulua and Tabasco, exchanging all they had for cacao and stone beads."[18]

> "The occupation to which [the Maya] had the greatest inclination was trade, carrying salt and cloth and slaves to the land of Ulua and Tabasco, exchanging all they had for cacao and stone beads."[18]
>
> —Spanish monk Diego de Landa

Recent archaeological excavations at Tikal demonstrate the value and extent of this commerce. Tikal, a powerful city-state in what is now northern Guatemala, was built on land that had plentiful deposits of flint, a stone useful for starting fires and for toolmaking. Despite the abundance of flint, though, Tikal lacked other important raw materials. Most notably, the region around the city has no naturally occurring supplies of obsidian, a thin, sharp, black rock often used for cutting. Nonetheless, archaeologists have

Much of Maya trade was carried out among the city-states that made up the Maya territory. For the most part, salt produced near the Yucatán seacoast was consumed by other Maya groups further inland. And obsidian and other rocks were mined in one corner of the Maya homeland and traded to parts of the region where obsidian was unavailable. But the Maya also took part in long-distance trade with neighboring peoples. Several important trade routes ran through Maya territory on their way to cultures to the south and the west of the Maya, and the Maya used these routes to exchange goods with these cultures as well.

Indeed, these external trade routes probably did a great deal to enrich the Maya and increase their economic and political power. As one source notes, "As intermediaries between Mexico and Central America, and as producers of highly desirable resources (jadeite, obsidian, salt, quetzal feathers, and much more), the Maya were inescapably the middlemen and the masters of much of the Mesoamerican economic system." Not only did intercultural trade bring the Maya goods they could not produce themselves, but their position at the center of the trade routes enabled them to dictate what goods they would allow to pass through their territory—thus helping them control the commerce of the entire region.

Robert J. Sharer and Loa P. Traxler, *The Ancient Maya*, 6th ed. Palo Alto, CA: Stanford University Press, 2006, p. 84.

found plenty of obsidian blades in and around the ruins of Tikal. All evidence indicates that these pieces of obsidian originated from natural deposits of the rock in highland regions hundreds of miles away. Evidently, the citizens of Tikal traded pieces of flint they did not need for obsidian they could not produce on their own. Through this commerce, the people of Tikal improved their own lives and the lives of their trading partners as well.

If the Maya homeland had been entirely rain forest or exclusively mountainous, then each part of the region would have been equally able to find its own raw materials or produce its own crops. In that case there would have been little need for trade, as no Maya group would have had anything that another lacked. The commerce that marked the classic period was a natural product of the differences in landforms and climate that prevailed across the area. In this model, people in one region exchanged their excess goods and resources for the materials that they could not make or find on their own.

The decisions in the Maya world about what crops to plant and what goods to trade for were based on a variety of factors, including individual choice. Maya farmers used the best methods they knew to create productive cropland out of the wilderness; merchants bought and sold whatever goods they thought would bring them the most wealth. But even individual choice was based on the conditions imposed on the Maya by their climate and their geography. Slash-and-burn agriculture was a natural response to the poor soils prevalent in the Maya Tropical Forest, just as terrace agriculture worked well on the sloping hills and mountains of the highlands. The need for salt, limestone, feathers, and other raw and finished goods drove the Maya to create an extensive trade network that benefited everyone. The Maya's characteristic agricultural techniques and patterns of trade were a direct response to the geographic realities of the world in which they made their home.

CHAPTER THREE

How Did Religion Affect Maya Art and Science?

Focus Questions

1. Do you think that Maya scientists would have preferred to study science for the sake of science, rather than studying science as an arm of religion? Why or why not?
2. What advantages and disadvantages are there for a society in making art subservient to religious ideals? Explain your thinking.
3. What, in your opinion, are some of the most defining aspects of the Maya religion? Explain your answer.

It is almost impossible to consider Maya society without reference to the Maya religion. Members of the nobility were not just temporal leaders; they were considered minor divinities who might eventually become full-fledged gods following their deaths. Priests wielded great political power and held high social status as well. Certain plants and animals, such as cacao beans, tobacco, and the quetzal bird, were imbued with religious significance, and cities, even small ones, constructed elaborate temples for use in worship. The gods— and there were dozens of them, each with his or her own sphere of responsibility—were deeply involved in the lives of Maya commoners and nobles alike. Very little was more central to Maya identity and society than the religion of the Maya people. "Every aspect of the life of every Maya, from the lowliest peasant to the most exalted ruler," write authors Carolyn Meyer and Charles Gallenkamp, "was tied to rituals and sacred symbols."[19]

The importance of religion to the Maya had several significant effects. Most notably, spiritual ideas often dictated how Maya leaders and com-

The flamboyant long-tailed quetzal bird (shown) was one of the many jungle creatures imbued with religious significance by the Maya.

moners behaved. The question of precisely when crop planting should begin, for example, could be answered by divination—that is, through religious rituals conducted by priests. Whether to wage a war against a nearby enemy was often less a military decision than a spiritual one, as religious leaders tried to determine if the gods would look favorably on such an undertaking. The selection of the next ruler of a city-state, similarly, might be as much a religious decision as a political one, as those in charge of making the choice looked for the alternative that the gods seemed to support. In dozens of ways, great and small, the religious ideas of the Maya shaped the way the people of the region lived their lives.

That was especially true of two areas of Maya society: art and science. The Maya were expert artists and craftspeople who produced exceptionally beautiful carvings, sculptures, and murals. Similarly, they had a deep understanding of many aspects of science, especially astronomy and mathematics. Modern Americans largely accept that art and science have specific functions: In very general terms, art is intended to bring beauty to the world, and science is designed to help people understand the workings of the universe. The Maya, however, had a different perspective. In their view, art objects and scientific understanding were both fundamentally aspects of religion. Art was created not so much for aesthetic purposes, but to please the gods and to strengthen the connections between gods and earthly rulers. In the same way, scientific discovery was less about knowledge for its own sake than about determining how best to understand the connection of the spiritual to the here and now. More than any other aspect of Maya life, Maya art and science were shaped by religious beliefs.

> "In its complexity and subtlety, in its sheer volume and innovation, Maya art is the greatest of New World art styles."[20]
>
> —Art historian Mary Ellen Miller

The Art of the Maya

Any list of the finest achievements of the Maya would include objects of art. Indeed, some experts go even further in their praise: "In its complexity and subtlety," writes art historian Mary Ellen Miller, "in its sheer volume and innovation, Maya art is the greatest of New World art styles."[20] Today art galleries far from Central America own extensive collections of Maya art. In the United States, for instance, museums in cities such as Philadelphia, Chicago, and New York are known for their selection of Maya artworks. Elsewhere in the world, visitors to Japan, Switzerland, and other countries can find impressive examples of art created by Maya jewelers, stone carvers, and others.

As Miller suggests, the art of the Maya encompassed a variety of styles and forms. Perhaps the best known of these today is sculpture. "Sculpture for the ancient Maya spans all media, from the miniature to the monumental,"[21] notes museum curator James Doyle. Some sculptors used obsidian blades and other tools to carve wood, jade, and bone into intricate figurines. Others used limestone and other varieties of rock to fashion life-size statues. In addition to bone, stone, and wood, sculptors made use of clay and shells as raw materials for their sculptures. Today most wooden sculptures from the classic period no longer exist, having rotted years ago in the hot, wet climate of the Central American lowlands; but many examples of sculpture, both large and small, created from other materials remain.

Related to sculptures were stone monuments known as stelae. Typically 12 to 13 feet (3.7 to 4 m) high, Maya stelae were most often made from limestone. Most stelae were covered with carvings that frequently depicted human figures. "The front was the figure of a man curiously and richly dressed," wrote nineteenth-century explorer John Lloyd Stephens upon encountering a stela for the first time, "and the face, evidently a portrait, [was] solemn, stern, and well fitted to excite terror."[22] The bulk of stelae depict the faces of monarchs. Most include glyphs as well, which list some of the monarchs' most important achievements.

Painting was another artistic discipline in which the Maya excelled. Many, though not all, Maya paintings took on the form of murals, which were typically painted on the plaster walls of palaces, temples, and other large buildings. The subject matter of murals ranged from lords and gods to battle scenes and depictions of daily life. Most of these murals have long since vanished; like wooden sculptures, the humidity has caused many of them to disintegrate. Nonetheless, some do survive, and they are widely considered to be remarkable accomplishments. "It is really breathtaking how beautiful this is,"[23] says archaeologist William Saturno about a mural in the modern-day city of San Bartolo in Guatemala.

Gods and Monarchs

Maya artworks of the classic period cover an assortment of topics: animals of the rain forest, human figures, geometric designs, and much more. The most common subjects of Maya art, however, are gods and

This jade mask is evidence of the skills wielded by Maya artisans. The most common subjects for art were the gods and the Maya rulers.

earthly rulers. This was not an accident. The Maya believed that the gods were fundamentally responsible for whatever happened in human affairs. Each god controlled some aspect of human existence, good or bad. Among the most important was Kinich Ajaw, a sun god who, according to author Leonard Everett Fisher, "brought good health and happiness to his people."[24] Other examples include Ix Chel, a goddess who governed flooding, the phases of the moon, and childbirth; Xaman Ek, who was said to take a particular interest in the well-being of travelers; and dozens more.

Since architecture is in a sense a combination of art and science, it is unsurprising that it was another area in which the Maya excelled. Palaces, temples, and pyramids rose above the surrounding cityscapes, sometimes reaching heights above 200 feet (61 m). Made mostly of limestone with white stucco covering, these buildings reflected the sunlight, making them stand out further. Courtyards, plazas, and stairways, also fashioned of stone, connected the temples and palaces. The city centers of communities such as Palenque and Tikal rivaled anything in Europe during the centuries of the classic period.

Like Maya art and science, Maya architecture was also heavily influenced by religious ideas. Though the palaces where rulers lived were often quite large, temples tended to be even bigger. Certainly the construction of temples took up a sizable share of the royal treasury. Moreover, Maya buildings often included religious carvings and icons, such as depictions of sacred animals; serpent masks, used in various rituals, were common decorations in temples. Other religious features appeared in Maya architecture as well. The Maya underworld was believed to consist of nine layers, for example, and many Maya temples and pyramids had nine exterior levels to reflect the structure of the underworld. Even secular buildings such as palaces had clear connections to religion. The buildings of the Nunnery complex, a royal residence in a city called Uxmal, have different numbers of doorways, with the numbers corresponding to numbers important in the Maya religion.

Many artworks therefore depicted individual gods or objects associated with them, such as sacred animals of the rain forest. A palace in the city of Kabah, for example, featured dozens of carvings of a powerful god named Itzamna. Yum Kaax, the god of maize, or corn, got particularly positive treatment in the art of the Maya. He was usually shown as handsome and young, his hair thin and light like the silk of an ear of corn. "The Maya Maize God embodied human perfection,"[25] notes Miller. Upon seeing these depictions, religious authorities believed, gods such as Itzamna and Yum Kaax would be moved to favor the people who created them. In this way the religious sentiments and traditions of the Maya guided them to create art that—they hoped—would influence the all-powerful gods, whose whims had an enormous effect on the world.

The prevalence of images of royalty is likewise explained by the religious feelings of the Maya. According to tradition, rulers were deities, and Maya art often reflected—and emphasized—that connection. Paintings and sculptures that depict earthly kings and queens, for instance, often show the ruler with clothing or facial features popularly associated with certain gods. A carved stone from the city-state of Kaminaljuyu is one example. Not only does the carving depict a king who is dressed to look like a bird god, but the stone shows him floating in space above the earth—an indication that the king should be viewed as something more than strictly human.

Indeed, kings and queens were popularly expected to travel to the underworld, a mythical place known as Xibalba, after death, and many artworks depicted these journeys in great detail—perhaps to remind viewers that the rulers were not simply people. The lid of the sarcophagus created for a king named K'inich Janaab' Pakal (or Pacal), for instance, was decorated with symbols representing Xibalba. "The intricately carved sarcophagus lid," writes religious scholar David Carrasco, "depicted the image of the Maya cosmos and Pacal's journey through it."[26] It is likely that the unknown artist who designed the lid was aware of creating a thing of beauty. Even so, the main purpose of this piece of art was religious. The beauty was largely if not exclusively a means to an end—in this case the goal of making sure that the king's status as a minor divinity was properly recognized.

Astronomy, Math, and the Calendar

If the Maya were skilled in art, their understanding of science—especially astronomy, math, and calendars—was perhaps even more noteworthy. The Maya of the classic period probably had a more advanced grasp of astronomy than any other civilization on the planet at the time. Maya understanding of mathematics was equally strong, especially as compared to other peoples of the time, and the Maya calendar was extremely sophisticated. Sylvanus Morley, an early expert on Maya culture, argued that the Maya understanding of astronomy represented "the highest intellectual achievement"[27] in the New World prior to the arrival of the Spanish.

The Maya certainly had a deep interest in the motions of the stars and the planets. Without any advanced equipment—the Maya never invented tools such as telescopes or even binoculars—Maya astronomers carefully charted the appearances of different celestial bodies in the sky. They recorded their observations, looked for patterns, and used what they learned to further their understanding of the heavens. The astronomers' ability to make sense of their observations was remarkable. Long before the end of the classic period, the Maya had accurately calculated the length of the year to the third decimal place (their figure was 365.2420 days; the correct figure is 365.2422), and knew how to predict precisely when the next lunar eclipse would occur.

The Maya's mathematical achievements were likewise impressive. Maya mathematicians developed a number system that relied on place value, much like the decimal system used throughout the world today. In the Maya system, different symbols represented different numbers. A dot, for example, represented the number 1, while a line stood for 5. The symbols could be combined, moreover, to create other numbers. To show 13, for instance, the Maya would draw two lines (2 x 5, or 10) and three dots (3 x 1, or 3). Most important, the Maya used a zero as a placeholder as we do today; this enabled them to write even large numbers with only a handful of symbols, in the same way as including extra zeros enables modern mathematicians to distinguish large numbers such as 400,000 from small numbers such as 40 or even 4. In contrast to the Maya, the ancient Greeks, Romans, and Egyptians, among many other advanced civilizations, never developed the idea of a zero.

But perhaps the crowning scientific achievement of the Maya was their calendar, which Meyer and Gallenkamp describe as "probably the most accurate . . . ever devised by an ancient civilization."[28] The Maya calendar was certainly accurate; it was also extraordinarily intricate. It consisted of two cycles, one with 260 days and the other with 365. Within each cycle, each day was given a name and a number, similar to the way we might write September 29 or May 11 today. Because the cycles ran concurrently, any given day had two of these modifiers; thus,

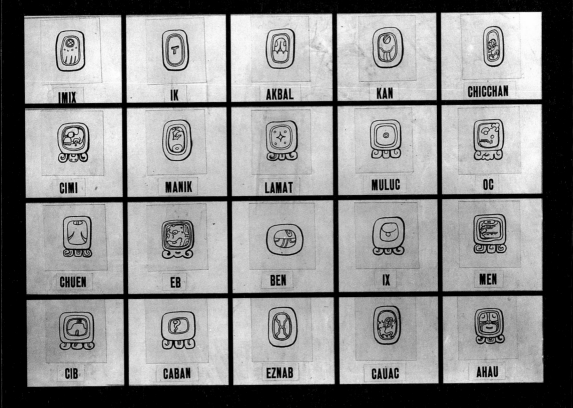

The incredibly accurate and complex Maya calendar gave each day a name and a number. This chart shows their pictograms of the names of the days.

a day might be referred to as 2 Ahau 5 Kumku. The calendar measured time in units of days, years, and beyond. A *tun*, for example, was 7,200 days, or about 20 years. But even that figure was dwarfed by a *baktun*, which was 2,880,000 days—about 8,000 years.

Science and Worship

Some of the Maya interest in science and the calendar came from everyday concerns. The Maya certainly benefited from having an accurate calendar that could help them determine when to plant and when to harvest, for example. Similarly, Maya merchants no doubt appreciated their culture's number system when they were calculating prices and income. A second potential motivation for the Maya interest in science, at least among those who gathered data and interpreted the findings, may have involved the intellectual challenge of making

The Maya Underworld

Maya religious life was distinctive in part for its complex view of the underworld, a place the Maya knew as Xibalba. Maya mythology described Xibalba in great detail. As archaeologists Linda Schele and David Freidel explain, "Xibalba had animals, plants, inhabitants of various kinds, and a landscape with both natural and constructed features." However, Xibalba was neither friendly nor welcoming. The main inhabitants of Xibalba were a group of gods known collectively as the Lords of Death, who were unpleasant at best and lethal at worst.

The Maya believed that Xibalba was a real place, connected to the earth by a road; in fact, Maya tradition held that certain caves in parts of the Yucatán marked the earthly end of the trail. The way was long and difficult, however; those who wanted to travel to Xibalba were forced to cross a river of blood, then traverse another river of pus and make their way through several other obstacles. Only after death, Maya tradition held, would anyone make a journey to Xibalba.

Linda Schele and David Freidel, *A Forest of Kings: The Untold Story of the Ancient Maya*. New York: Morrow, 1990, p. 66.

predictions about the sky or investigating large numbers. Archaeologist Berthold Riese argues that the sheer complexity of Maya math indicates a "thirst for knowledge" along with a "desire to explore the limits of [the Maya] mathematical system."[29]

For the most part, though, the Maya did not engage in these areas of study for practical reasons or to satisfy their intellectual curiosity. As was the case with art, Maya interest in calendars, astronomy, and math was mainly a result of their interest in religion. "Astronomy," writes anthropologist Heather McKillop, "was integrally linked to religion in that the Maya believed that the sun, moon, planets, and stars were gods who impacted, and in some cases, controlled, human destiny."[30] The calendar, similarly, was constructed to allow Maya priests to identify auspicious and inauspicious days and times of the year for certain activities. Each day and group of days was associated with a given god or group of deities, and priests read and interpreted the calendar to see what lay ahead. When good gods were well represented on the calendar, the priests reported that good times would be coming; when evil gods were ascendant, the opposite was true. In this sense the Maya calendar functioned much as the signs of the zodiac function for modern astrologers.

Astronomy, too, was a direct outgrowth of Maya religious thinking. Along with a deep understanding of mathematics, the knowledge the Maya had of astronomy was necessary to help them develop an accurate calendar. In addition, Maya astronomy reflected and supported the Maya's spiritual beliefs. The Milky Way, for example, was believed to be the embodiment of the World Tree, or Tree of Life, which was an important image in Maya mythology. By charting the position of the Milky Way in the night sky, Maya astronomers were in effect honoring—and keeping track of—the tree, not just paying attention to the movements of the stars. To the Maya, moreover, the day itself was a religious representation of human life and death. As Robert J. Sharer points out, "The sun was born at dawn for a brief life span across the sky, only to be swallowed in death by the underworld at dusk."[31]

Religion was at the heart of some of the Maya's greatest achievements. Indeed, what the Maya accomplished in both art and science could very often be traced back to ideas of religion. Maya religion affected art, with Maya paintings, sculptures, and buildings focusing heavily on religious imagery, mythology, and the connection between the here and now and the afterlife. Maya religion similarly shaped scientific thinking, with the goal being the development of intricate calendars that could be used to determine what the gods were thinking. In this way Maya religious beliefs and practices deeply influenced both science and art.

"The sun was born at dawn for a brief life span across the sky, only to be swallowed in death by the underworld at dusk."[31]

—Archaeologist Robert J. Sharer

CHAPTER FOUR

How Did Trade Help Unify Maya Society?

Focus Questions

1. In your opinion, what was the greatest single benefit that trade provided to the Maya—and why?
2. Besides trade and political unity, in what other ways might the various peoples of a culture be brought together? Explain your answer.
3. What role did specialized manufacturing play in creating a single Maya culture? Give reasons to support your thinking.

Trade was a vital part of the Maya civilization during the classic period. Well-traveled trade routes wound along the coasts and up and down the rivers of the region. Marketplaces dotted the big cities and smaller towns alike. A merchant class organized and regularized commerce, ensuring that goods could be brought from almost any point within Maya territory to almost any other point. Though the Maya made extensive use of barter, in which one commodity was exchanged for another, the Maya economy eventually became sophisticated enough that cacao beans and other goods were used as money. To the Maya of the classic period, indeed, commerce was very nearly a national obsession. As Carolyn Meyer and Charles Gallenkamp wryly describe it, "When the Maya weren't fighting, they were trading."[32]

This emphasis on commerce benefited the Maya in several ways. Most obviously, trade allowed city-states to provide their people with goods that would otherwise have been unavailable to them. A community without a local source of pearls, alabaster, or lime did not have to go without; instead, it could obtain the materials it needed through trade. In addition, trade provided a sort of safety net to the Maya of the classic period. If a harvest was bad in one part of the Guatemalan highlands, for instance, residents of the area might be able to make up the deficit by exchanging some of their supplies of limestone, artwork, or tools for another community's excess grain. And trade allowed some Maya—and some Maya city-states—to become quite wealthy. "The most important cities," writes Lynn V. Foster, "often controlled commodities or . . . [trade] routes."[33]

"When the Maya weren't fighting, they were trading."[32]

—Authors Carolyn Meyer and Charles Gallenkamp

There was another advantage to commerce, though: the value of trade in bringing the Maya together. The Maya, after all, had no political unity. No single emperor demanded allegiance from Maya peoples across the Yucatán and the Guatemalan highlands; no government imposed uniformity on highlanders and lowlanders alike. Under these circumstances, it would have been easy for the various peoples of the region to drift apart, with different groups developing distinctive artistic styles, varying architectural designs, and different symbols of wealth and status. That did not happen, however, and the primary reason is commerce. Given the Maya emphasis on markets, trade routes, and exchange, it was easy for goods and ideas to flow between different parts of the region. More than any other factor, the Maya passion for commerce helped create and sustain a truly Maya identity.

The Rise of Commerce

The emphasis on trade among the Maya began early. Long before the classic period began, goods were being exchanged within various parts of Maya territory: shells and salt from the coastal zones to inland communities, stones such as obsidian and alabaster from the highlands to the lowlands. Most likely, early commerce among the Maya was haphazard, with few established marketplaces or trade routes. An enterprising or needy villager might head up a river with some extra cacao beans or a handful of quetzal feathers and use these items to haggle with the next community upstream for surplus grain, animal pelts, or arrowheads. But these trips probably were not undertaken on any kind of regular schedule.

As Maya influence grew, though, so did trade. Trade routes sprang up across the Maya territory, most along water but some connecting to inland areas as well. "A southern route ran along the Pacific coastal plain," writes Robert J. Sharer, "and northern routes ran across the lowlands."[34] Marketplaces appeared as well in large cities and smaller villages alike, allowing people of all classes to buy and sell food, animals, stone, pottery, and much more. Some were open weekly or monthly, but others may have been in use on a daily basis. "Sacks of dry corn and beans abounded," writes Victoria Schlesinger, describing what these markets must have looked like. "Yards of fabric and yarns, the cotton coming from the Yucatan, were available for sewing."[35]

As the classic period went on, Maya society became more specialized. Workshops began to open in certain parts of the region to manufacture or mine different products. Anthropologist Arthur J. Mann

A Maya boat laden with cargo to trade approaches the shore in this depiction. The Maya's main trade routes followed the coastlines and rivers.

describes the system as a "regional division of labor"[36] in which certain cities or geographic zones were associated with a specific item, such as jade, limestone, or ceramics. In a few coastal regions, for example, the inhabitants constructed saltworks where large quantities of seawater were boiled or evaporated, thus isolating the salt. Part of the reason for these saltworks, of course, was to ensure a sufficient supply of salt for the people of that community, but it seems clear that the intention was also to trade excess salt for other goods less available in that part of the Maya territory.

Other areas similarly became known for different resources or technologies. The island of Wild Cane Cay off the coast of what is now Belize, for example, became a center for obsidian production. The Pacific coast of what is now Guatemala was known for its production of chocolate. Colha in modern-day Belize was a focal point for the making of stone tools. Various regions were instrumental in the manufacture of ceramics, the production of limestone, and the creation of textiles. No central authority pushed the Maya economy in the direction of specialization, but it certainly proved efficient to concentrate glassmaking in one part of Maya territory and the production of cotton in another. It also proved lucrative for the manufacturers; if they could produce the best—and most—of any given material, they would be able to charge correspondingly high prices for it.

> "Sacks of dry corn and beans abounded. Yards of fabric and yarns, the cotton coming from the Yucatan, were available for sewing."[35]
>
> —Author Victoria Schlesinger, describing Maya marketplaces

Jade

In ways both large and small, the commerce that characterized Maya society of the classic period served to bring the Maya people together. An excellent example involves jade, the semiprecious stone that served as the basis for a myriad of Maya sculptures and figurines. In addition to its use in sculpture, jade was particularly important in religious rituals, including those that dealt with the dead. Decorations made from jade often appeared on the tombs of important people, for example. In addition, jade was widely used by members of the nobility to emphasize their riches and their rank. "Wealthy people liked to have bits of jade inset in their front teeth as a mark of social prestige,"[37] explain Meyer and Gallenkamp.

Indeed, jade is probably more closely associated with the Maya today than any other object. Every modern museum featuring Maya art displays jade sculptures as part of its collection; books about the Maya often feature jade art on their covers. The use of jade, notably, is not generally connected with any specific areas of the Maya homelands. Pendants, sculptures, and other art objects from cities as widely scattered as Copan in the southeast and Palenque in the northwest were made from jade. Priests in inland and coastal areas alike made use of jade in carrying out certain rites. Rich nobles across the region outfitted their bodies with jade to display their status. Though supplies of

Controlling Trade

While the Maya had no overarching political system, local rulers held absolute power throughout most of the region. These monarchs oversaw many aspects of life within their city-states, choosing when to go to war, what construction projects to undertake, and so on. In most cases trade was one of the areas they controlled. Rulers took stock of the natural resources and manufactured products available in their own city-states and determined how much of each could be exchanged in trade with other groups. They controlled the supply of these items as well to ensure the highest possible price; it would be foolish to sell too much limestone or too many jaguar pelts at the same time, since prices would drop.

Control of trade enriched the leaders—especially as they most likely took a percentage of the profits from every transaction—and helped them consolidate their authority within their territory. However, it also led to greater standardization of the products available in the Maya world. It was in the interest of rulers to make their cities known for specific products, and in their interests as well to make sure these goods were sturdy and well made. Thus, the obsidian, arrowheads, or textiles the merchants of a given city-state offered for sale most likely met a certain level of quality. Especially as trade networks grew more complex, this informal version of quality control ensured that similar items were being exchanged across the entire region.

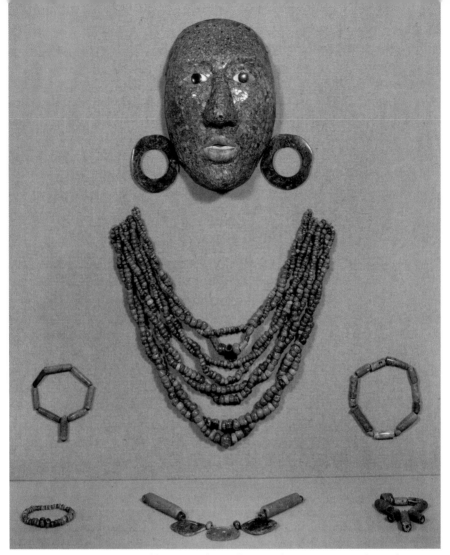

Jade, used to create artifacts such as these adornments and mask, was one of the most highly traded commodities among the Maya.

jade were limited—it would not have been so valuable had it been easy to obtain—it appeared everywhere in the region.

Yet like many other natural resources, jade is not evenly distributed throughout Central America. In fact, the great bulk of Maya territory is and was devoid of jade. All the jade used by the classic period Maya came ultimately from the Motagua River valley in what is now Guatemala. Residents of this valley mined the stone, which was then carried by traders along the Motagua River and overland to urban centers such as Tikal and Palenque. There the jade was exchanged for other goods. Commerce therefore made the wide distribution of jade possible—and allowed jade to become a symbol of the entire Maya world, not just a symbol of the people who lived near that specific river.

The spread of jade throughout the Yucatán and beyond was helpful in forming the Maya people into a single culture. But the connection between the different parts of the Maya world was not just about everyone having the same material. Rather, it had to do with the way that material was used. "The movement of goods," writes Sharer, "also implies the movement of ideas."[38] Thus, not only was the jade the same from one end of Maya territory to the other, but the rituals that involved jade were similar, the decorations crafted from jade were similar—whether on tombs or on teeth—and the artistic styles and values related to jade sculptures were essentially the same as well. Through the buying and selling of jade, the Maya disseminated a material throughout their homeland—and disseminated a way of life as well.

> "The movement of goods also implies the movement of ideas."[38]
>
> —Archaeologist Robert J. Sharer

Feathers, Pelts, and Limestone

Jade was one frequently traded material that came to symbolize the Maya all through the Yucatán and beyond. It was not, however, the only one. Many other materials exchanged among the Maya also helped bring the peoples of the land together. Items that were often used as luxury goods for noblemen and noblewomen were especially good examples of how commerce could spread ideas and lead to greater cultural cohesion. Quetzal feathers, for instance, were used throughout the Maya world to indicate royalty. There is evidence, in fact, that no one other than monarchs and their immediate families were permitted to wear these feathers, which could easily grow to be over 3 feet (about 1 m) long. Even within royal families, the number of feathers could mark gradations of importance. "The prince," wrote a Spanish observer many years after the classic period had come to a close, "had three canopies [of feathers] and the other brothers or sons, two."[39]

As with jade, though, the feathers of the quetzal were not available everywhere in Maya territory. Rather, quetzals lived mainly in the forests of the highlands and tended to avoid low-lying areas. Nonetheless, because of the Maya expertise in setting up and maintaining trade routes and marketplaces, rulers along the coasts had no difficulty securing the feathers they craved so they could properly demonstrate their political power and status. Trade not only distributed these feathers across the region but made it so the feathers carried the same

This statue of a Maya noble still shows the green coloring on his shield and headdress that depicts quetzal feathers. The feathers were a major trade item, as they were used to show a person's social status.

message—the wearer of these objects is of royal blood—regardless of where in Maya territory they were.

Other luxury items also reveal how the extensive commercial networks of the Maya served to provide specific goods to every monarch or noble. Jaguar pelts came largely from the rain forest, for example, but found their way to every corner of the region. But not all of these goods were luxury items for the elite. In the same way that jade characterizes Maya sculpture, so too does limestone serve as a symbol for the architecture of the society. The exterior limestone walls of palaces and temples are aesthetically pleasing, and photos of the massive public buildings constructed by the Maya are easy to find—often on

The Market in Chunchucmil

Archaeologists have spent countless hours over the years investigating the palaces and temples of the Maya city-states, but investigation of other structures has been much more difficult. The main reason for this is simply that the public buildings were crafted from limestone, which erodes slowly; thus, the buildings are still standing centuries later. In contrast, ordinary houses, markets, and other less imposing structures were typically made from wood, which is much less permanent.

In recent years, though, researchers have used complex chemical analysis and other advanced techniques to identify where open-air marketplaces, in particular, might have stood. In 2007 archaeologists exploring the Yucatán city of Chunchucmil found evidence of a marketplace that had been used during the classic period. The market was located on a footpath, and staple foods such as corn and beans were certainly among the items exchanged. "Just who traded in the marketplace is not known," says one of the archaeologists, but the evidence suggests that both the residents of Chunchucmil and visiting merchants were involved in commerce at the site. The discovery was an exciting one in the world of Maya scholarship and has led to new efforts to identify and investigate other potential market sites across the Maya territory.

Quoted in Kelly Hearn, "Ancient Maya Marketplace Found," *National Geographic*, December 4, 2007. http://news.nationalgeographic.com.

book and magazine covers that do not feature jade figurines. Because of the far-flung network of trade routes Maya merchants developed, it simply did not matter that limestone was not available everywhere in Maya territory. Those peoples who did not have easy access to limestone could exchange other goods for the stones they wanted. As a result, there is a striking similarity among the public buildings, plazas, and staircases constructed by various Maya groups: Not only are they all manufactured from the same type of stone, but they all look much alike.

Indirect Effects of Trade

Many factors contributed to the cohesion of the Maya as a culture and as a single society, and commerce was not the only one. The choice of corn, squash, and beans as the three major crops grown by essentially every group within the Maya world was largely due to the geographic conditions that favored the growth of these plants. The fact that the same mythology prevailed from the Atlantic to the Pacific and from the lowlands to the highlands was mainly attributable to the power of narrative and the oral tradition. No one put the Maya calendar up for sale, exchanged mathematical knowledge between city-states, or bought and sold ideas for religious rituals—to name three features of Maya society widely shared among all the Maya peoples. Nor were city designs spread through commerce, and yet, as T. Patrick Culbert notes, "all Mayan cities [are] much alike in basic layout."[40] Not everything was fundamentally about trade.

But even features such as agriculture, science, and religion were indirectly affected by the Maya thirst for commerce. By creating trade routes to carry goods to and from the distant outposts of Maya territory, the Maya were enabling communication between different groups. When merchants from one city-state reached a faraway port, they brought valuable commodities. But they also brought new ideas: a more efficient way of farming on a hillside, information about a recent discovery of an omen in the night sky, even a new style of clothing never seen before in that part of the world. By the same token, they took back what they saw and experienced while away from home. In this way the very existence of commerce encouraged the flow of ideas from one community or city-state to another. When one group of Maya adopted the styles, interests, or designs of other Maya groups, they were helping consolidate the culture and bring its people closer together.

Then again, the realities of life in the Maya world made it difficult for cohesion to spread in any other way. Other New World civilizations, notably those of the South American Inca and the Aztec of Mexico, were structured differently from the Maya: While the Inca and Aztec had developed a powerful political empire to go along with their cultural identity, the Maya did not. Indeed, the Maya had no central government beyond the level of the city-state. While Palenque, Tikal, or Copan each had its own powerful leaders, there was no overarching monarch ranking above those kings and queens.

In the case of the Inca or the Aztec—or for that matter the Romans or ancient Egyptians of the Old World—the presence of an emperor meant that much could be mandated throughout the kingdom. An emperor could command that everyone use the same form of money, for instance, or pressure lower-ranking leaders to force builders to use a particular architectural style for public buildings. In the world of the Maya, though, that was not possible, as the city-states were independent. Short of fighting a potentially disastrous war, which few Maya city-states chose to wage, no one in Caracol or Tikal had any ability to make the people of another city do anything at all.

Keeping Maya society cohesive was not a task for the political elites. What most closely linked Maya communities together was in fact the merchants, the marketplaces, and the extensive trade routes that ran through the lands of the Maya. By exchanging goods—and whether they knew it or not, knowledge and information—Maya traders succeeded in bringing Maya society closer together. They spread their cultural values and created a surprising unity among very different groups. In the end, the Maya did not need the presence of an emperor or even the existence of a political nation to establish a truly Maya society. All they needed was trade.

CHAPTER FIVE

How Did Environmental Issues Contribute to the Collapse of Maya Society?

Focus Questions

1. How compelling do you find the explanation that drought caused the Maya collapse—and why?
2. What factors drove the Maya to increase their use of slash-and-burn agriculture, and what were the consequences of these actions?
3. How and why did geography lead to the collapse of Maya civilization?

The classic period of the Maya civilization lasted for hundreds of years. Beginning in about 250 CE and stretching for more than six centuries, the Maya were at the peak of their powers during this time. Culturally, economically, and politically, they were unquestionably the dominant people of Central America. Their art, their scientific understanding, the complexity of their social organization, and their sophisticated trade systems all outpaced the achievements of nearby peoples. Indeed, the Maya of the classic period may well have constructed the most advanced civilization anywhere in the New World during these years.

Then, around 900 CE, the classic period came to a sudden end, to be replaced by a time of considerably lowered economic and artistic productivity. During this era, known today as the postclassic period, builders more or less stopped constructing temples, palaces, pyramids, and other large structures. Sculptors and painters no longer created as many works, and most experts agree that the quality of what they did produce began to diminish. The largest Maya urban areas, such as Tikal and Palenque, underwent a dramatic loss of population at this time as well. In the span of a generation or two, some of these cities had become essentially abandoned. "Grass overtook the courtyards," writes Charles Gallenkamp, "vines and the spreading roots of trees crept into doorways. . . . Within a century the jungle had reclaimed the ill-destined cities of the Maya."[41] The few cities that were not completely deserted were much smaller—and far less influential—than they had been.

> "Within a century the jungle had reclaimed the ill-destined cities of the Maya."[41]
>
> —Author Charles Gallenkamp

It would be an exaggeration to say that Maya culture disappeared entirely around 900. In fact, some elements of the classic period civilization continued to flourish, even following the cessation of large-scale construction projects and the dwindling population of the cities. That was especially true in certain areas of the northern Yucatán. Indeed, a few experts strenuously resist the notion that there was any kind of a collapse of the civilization around 900. Nonetheless, the evidence strongly indicates that Maya culture underwent significant political, artistic, and economic changes at the end of the classic period. And the great majority of scholars agree that after that point, the civilization was never again as dominant or as prosperous as it once had been. Scholar Michael D. Coe spoke for many when he wrote that the downfall of the Maya civilization represents "one of the most profound social and demographic catastrophes of all time."[42]

Theories of the Maya Demise

Today no one knows exactly what factors brought the classic period to an end. Over the years researchers have offered any number of theories—close to one hundred by at least one count—but no hypothesis has been accepted as definitive. Some have suggested, for example, that military conquest was the main cause of the collapse of the civilization. In this theory, invaders from elsewhere in Central America attacked and defeated Maya armies, replacing the thriving Maya culture with a less sophisticated one. Another possibility is that an epidemic spread throughout the region, killing hundreds of thou-

This lithograph shows the ruins of an abandoned Maya city overgrown by the jungle. For reasons still unclear, the Maya almost completely abandoned their cities within the span of a couple of generations.

sands of people. A deadly disease would certainly account for the depopulation of cities; it would also help explain why the big construction projects stopped, as the surviving labor force would not have been sufficient to build the massive stoneworks of the previous era.

Others have suggested that squabbles between various city-states interfered with commerce, affecting the Maya's ability to obtain the goods they needed to keep their civilization going as it had for years. Certainly, if limestone were suddenly made unavailable to lowland cities, for example, construction of large public buildings such as temples

A Growing Population

Population figures are difficult to determine for any ancient civilization. That is particularly true of cultures like that of the Maya, which did not enumerate their citizens—or at least did not record specific numbers anywhere. Nonetheless, historians and archaeologists have developed some useful tools for making estimates of the number of people who lived in the Maya homelands during the classic period. In the case of the Maya, these tools all indicate that the number of Maya rose throughout the first millennium CE. "Population growth was tremendous during the Classic Period," sums up Heather McKillop.

Indeed, the evidence strongly suggests that population rose especially sharply in the years leading up to the collapse. In the Copan Valley in what is now Honduras, for example, some researchers believe that the population was doubling every eighty years or so until the collapse. The population of Palenque in Mexico probably did not grow as rapidly as the population of Copan, but it does seem to have increased at a steady pace. The same is true of other cities. As the population grew, of course, the problems associated with feeding everyone would have become significantly greater. Without this population growth, it is possible that the collapse of the early 900s could have been averted.

Heather McKillop, *The Ancient Maya: New Perspectives*. Santa Barbara, CA: ABC-CLIO, 2004, p. 310.

and palaces would have been severely impacted. Archaeologist Robert J. Sharer has even suggested that the collapse may have been something of a self-fulfilling prophecy. In his hypothesis, Maya priests and astronomers of the late 800s searched the stars and found indications that the gods were going to bring Maya prosperity to an end. When warfare, disease, or disruption of trade began to affect the economic and political well-being of the civilization, Sharer theorizes, the Maya chose not to intervene by trying to stave off disaster. "It would be futile," Sharer explains, for the Maya "to challenge prophecies that foretold fundamental changes in their society."[43]

The archaeological record, however, does not strongly support any of these theories. There is no direct evidence of an invasion by other Central American armies, for example, and no clear indication that the trade routes dried up before, rather than after, the collapse of Maya civilization. Similarly, though the Maya of the classic period certainly experienced disease, mostly intestinal infections spread by parasites and insects, no one has demonstrated the presence of any epidemic so widespread or deadly as to bring about the collapse of civilization. Thus, the thinking among scholars today is that disease, trade, warfare, or fatalism may have contributed in small ways to the collapse, but they were not primary causes of the end of the classic period.

Mosquito-borne diseases would have been common in the jungle environment of the Maya. But no evidence can be found that a disease epidemic caused their civilization to disappear.

Instead, research on the causes of the collapse of Maya society is increasingly focused on the environment. In these scenarios, changes to landscapes, climate, and other aspects of the Maya natural world ultimately brought about the end of the classic period—and the end of Maya dominance in the region. If levels of rainfall dropped, for example, the society's ability to produce enough crops to feed its people might have been severely compromised. Food shortages, in turn, would have disrupted trade routes and could have led to brutal warfare between various city-states trying to control precious food supplies. Food shortages could likewise have sparked revolutions in which starving peasants struck against the ruling elites. In this way an environmental change could have had both direct and indirect consequences for the Maya, eventually leading to the collapse of the civilization.

Drought

For many years, scholars focused on drought as the most likely environmental cause of the Maya collapse. According to this perspective, rainfall in eastern Central America was steady and predictable through most of the classic period. While some years certainly brought less moisture than others, the amount of rainfall in most years was sufficient to replenish supplies of freshwater—and to enable Maya farmers to grow enough corn, beans, squash, and other crops to feed the people of the region. If not enough rain fell during any given year, hunger might be the immediate result. But Maya authorities could usually add to the food supply in a lean year by using food stored from previous growing seasons or by trading with peoples living in places where the drought had been less severe.

"Sunny days, in and of themselves, don't kill people. But when people run out of food and water, they die."[44]

—Archaeologist Richardson B. Gill

There is evidence that levels of rainfall across much of Central America may have dropped significantly, and for multiple years in a row, during the late 800s. In some parts of the Yucatán, the result could have been a drought that lasted a decade or more. Only those towns and villages situated along broad rivers, or those with access to deep wells, would have maintained an

This stand of corn has been decimated by drought. Some scientists believe an extended drought may have caused food and water shortages that led to the fall of Maya civilization.

adequate water supply during a time of drought. By most estimates, however, that included only about 5 percent of the Maya population. Sustained low rainfall could have essentially eliminated the freshwater resources for the great bulk of the Maya.

The effect of widespread drought on agriculture could have been just as damaging. Without sufficient rain, most crops wither and die. Corn, the most important Maya crop, is better able to withstand dry conditions than squash, beans, or other vegetables. But even in the case of corn, a lack of rain at certain critical points during the planting cycle can destroy the seedlings. Though the Maya were sometimes able to store extra grain for the future, they were not generally able to keep back more than a year's supply or so. Thus, a multiyear drought would have very quickly brought about a food shortage. "Sunny days, in and of themselves, don't kill people," writes archaeologist Richardson B. Gill, a leading proponent of the drought theory. "But when people run out of food and water, they die."[44]

Farming Techniques

Drought remains a popular explanation of the Maya collapse. In recent years, though, it has been gradually challenged by the notion that Maya agricultural practices were to blame for the end of the classic period. As archaeologist Tom Sever puts it, "They did it to themselves."[45] On the one hand, this seems like an odd idea. By the standards of the time, after all, the Maya were expert farmers. They knew how to use slash-and-burn agricultural techniques to carve farmland out of the rain forest. They recognized, moreover, that fields could be rejuvenated by allowing them to lie unused for a period of time. For centuries Maya agricultural techniques had provided an urbanized civilization with the food it required. Viewed in this light, attributing the Maya collapse to their farming methods appears unjustified.

> "They did it to themselves."[45]
>
> —Archaeologist Tom Sever

In other ways, however, Maya agriculture was problematic. In particular, slash-and-burn agriculture was remarkably inefficient. While burning stumps and bushes put nutrients into the soil and increased the yield of any given plot of land, the benefit was temporary. A single year of cultivation generally depleted the available nutrients. Farmers who tried to use the same plot of land two years in a row were invariably disappointed; not much came up, and what did grow was seldom worth the effort. "Once a field has been cultivated," writes Sharer, describing typical slash-and-burn methods used in Central America, "it must remain fallow to regain soil fertility—two or more years of fallow are required for each year of cultivation." The result, Sharer points out, is clear. "A third or less of the available farmland is cultivated in any given year," he concludes; "the bulk lies fallow."[46]

Depending on the number of people a culture needs to feed, large areas of unused land may not necessarily be a problem. In a subsistence society with a low population density and few nonfarmers, just a small fraction of potential farmland may well be enough to feed everyone. Even in a society with urban areas, allowing large stretches of land to remain fallow could still be acceptable. If trade routes are well established, as they were throughout most of Maya territory, it would be relatively easy to bring food from outlying farms into the cities to feed urban inhabitants. Indeed, through much of the classic period the agricultural techniques of the Maya, including slash-and-burn strategies, were probably sufficient to feed the people of the region on a regular basis.

But by the close of the classic period, the Maya population was becoming significantly larger—and more people meant more mouths to feed. As many experts view it today, the change in population resulted in important shifts in how the Maya thought about farming. It was one thing to leave fields lying fallow when the population was relatively low; but population growth made it increasingly difficult to justify leaving fields empty. Modern scholars increasingly argue that the Maya felt forced to abandon their long-term goal of ensuring that fields contained sufficient nutrients, even if that meant putting land out of service for a year or two, in favor of the short-term goal of feeding everyone by whatever means necessary. Given the larger population, farmers and planners felt pressure to plant crops in poor soil and hope that something came up, rather than let the field sit idle for a year or more.

A Growing Disaster

Similarly, through most of the classic period the Maya limited the number of fields they carved out of the rain forest. While Maya farmers of the time converted large swaths of forest to farmland, especially near cities, plenty of trees, bushes, and other vegetation remained. This was a wise choice for at least two reasons. First, there was no need for farmers to create more farmland while the population stayed relatively low, and therefore no point in putting in the work to make more fields. In addition, Maya farmers most likely knew that there were advantages to leaving extensive tracts of forest undisturbed. "Careful management, such as leaving large trees in place," writes Sharer, "allowed soils to recover more rapidly."[47] As the population grew, though, the Maya began converting more and more of the wilderness into arable land, cutting, clearing, and burning an ever-increasing area of forest to enable them to raise more crops.

The changes had a predictable effect. At first, the decision to plant in depleted soil simply resulted in extra work for relatively little gain, since farmers could not harvest nearly as much from the used-up fields as they could from land that had lain fallow. But as time went on, pressing fields into service for multiple years in a row actually began to reduce the amount of food that Maya farmers could produce. With fields given little opportunity to rest, the average yield of a plot of land began to drop. As yields from existing farmland decreased, in turn, more and more of the rain forest had to be turned into agricultural land to keep up with the burgeoning demand for food. This change, as Sharer notes, damaged the soil's fertility.

The situation would soon have worsened. Because tree roots serve to keep soil in place, undisturbed forest reduces erosion. As the Maya felled more and more trees in hopes of expanding cultivated land, more and more of the nutrients in the soil would have been washed away by rainfall. The Maya "ended up deforesting and destroying their landscape in efforts to eke out a living in hard times,"[48] explains archaeologist Robert Griffin. The result, as with the possibility of widespread drought, would have been lower crop yields, a dwindling food supply, and famine—which in turn would likely have led to civil unrest, violence, and perhaps open revolt. It is not difficult to see how carving a few too many farms out of the rain forest could eventually bring about the collapse of society.

The notion that Maya agricultural techniques were fundamentally responsible for the end of the classic period is gaining more and more acceptance among experts. Many researchers, however, still champion other causes for the Maya collapse, particularly the idea of drought. Some recent research suggests that the two explanations are linked. In this view, the Maya's overuse of slash-and-burn agriculture may have transformed the Central American climate and created conditions in which drought was likely. Rather than being the unlucky victims of shifts in weather patterns, the Maya unwittingly brought destruction on themselves. Studies run by National Aeronautics and Space Administration scientists and others suggest that large-scale removal of trees within the Yucatán region would have had a dramatic effect on the area's climate. In one model, notes Sever, the removal of the trees in the Maya homeland "caused a 3–5 degree rise in temperature and a 20–30 percent decrease in rainfall."[49]

The odds are good that the collapse of Maya civilization came about for multiple interrelated reasons. Warfare, civil unrest, disease, a breakdown of commerce—all are possibilities. But the evidence increasingly suggests that the root cause for the end of the classic period in Maya history had less to do with violence and economics and more

Collapse and Copan

Anthropologist Jared Diamond wrote about the downfall of the Maya civilization, among many others, in his book *Collapse*. In this excerpt, Diamond describes the process by which environmental degradation eventually led to the depopulation of the city of Copan.

> By the year A.D. 650, people started to occupy the hill slopes, but those hill sites were cultivated only for about a century. The percentage of Copan's total population that was in the hills, rather than in the valleys, reached a maximum of 41%, then declined until the population again became concentrated in the valley pockets. What caused that pullback of population from the hills? Excavation of the foundations of buildings in the valley floor showed that they became covered with sediment during the 8th century, meaning that the hill slopes were getting eroded and probably also leached of nutrients. Those acidic infertile hill soils were being carried down into the valley and blanketing the more fertile valley soils, where they would have reduced agricultural yields. . . .
>
> The reason for that erosion of the hillsides is clear: the forests that formerly covered them and protected their soils were being cut down. Dated pollen samples show that the pine forests originally covering the upper elevations of the hill slopes were eventually all cleared. Calculation suggests that most of those felled pine trees were being burned for fuel, while the rest were used for construction or for making plaster.

Jared Diamond, *Collapse*. New York: Viking Penguin, 2005.

to do with changes to the environment. Despite their skill at farming, despite their ability to flourish in the Central American climate and geography for hundreds of years, the time eventually came when the forests disappeared, the rains dried up, and the soil became exhausted. The Maya "knew their environment and how to survive within it,"[50] writes a journalist, but when those conditions changed, they could not adapt. In the long run, they were unable to defeat nature.

Introduction: The Maya World

1. Quoted in Inga Clendinnen, *Ambivalent Conquests: Maya and Spaniard in Yucatan, 1517–1570*. Cambridge: Cambridge University Press, 2003, p. 70.
2. Quoted in William Carlsen, "Ancient Mystery of Mayan Civilization," *SFGate*, September 12, 2004. www.sfgate.com.

Chapter One: A Brief History of the Ancient Maya

3. T. Patrick Culbert, *Maya Civilization*. Washington, DC: Smithsonian, 1993, p. 16.
4. John S. Henderson, *The World of the Ancient Maya*. Ithaca, NY: Cornell University Press, 1997, p. 23.
5. Henderson, *The World of the Ancient Maya*, p. 25.
6. Linda Schele and David Freidel, *A Forest of Kings: The Untold Story of the Ancient Maya*. New York: Morrow, 1990, p. 57.
7. Culbert, *Maya Civilization*, p. 59.
8. Quoted in Nigel Richardson, "Secret World of the Maya," *History Today*, May 2013. www.historytoday.com.
9. James Doyle, "Ancient Maya Sculpture," Metropolitan Museum of Art, 2016. www.metmuseum.org.
10. Schele and Freidel, *A Forest of Kings*, p. 91.

Chapter Two: How Did Geography Help Shape Maya Civilization?

11. Jared Diamond, "Geographic Determinism," Jared Diamond. www.jareddiamond.org.
12. Robert J. Sharer and Loa P. Traxler, *The Ancient Maya*, 6th ed. Palo Alto, CA: Stanford University Press, 2006, p. 29.
13. James D. Nations, *The Maya Tropical Forest: People, Parks, and Ancient Cities*. Austin: University of Texas Press, 2006, p. 45.
14. Quoted in Victor Wolfgang von Hagen, *The Aztec and Maya Papermakers*. Mineola, NY: Dover, 1999, p. 68.
15. Victoria Schlesinger, *Animals and Plants of the Ancient Maya: A Guide*. Austin: University of Texas Press, 2001, p. 53.

16. Lynn V. Foster, *Handbook to Life in the Ancient Maya World*. Oxford: Oxford University Press, 2005, p. 309.
17. Culbert, *Maya Civilization*, p. 18.
18. Quoted in Robert J. Sharer and David W. Sedat, *Archaeological Investigations of the Northern Maya Highlands: Guatemala*. Philadelphia: University of Pennsylvania Press, 1987, p. 450.

Chapter Three: How Did Religion Affect Maya Art and Science?

19. Carolyn Meyer and Charles Gallenkamp, *The Mystery of the Ancient Maya*, rev. ed. New York: Simon & Schuster, 1995, p. 58.
20. Mary Ellen Miller, *Maya Art and Architecture*. New York: Thames and Hudson, 1999, p. 11.
21. Doyle, "Ancient Maya Sculpture."
22. Quoted in Robert Wauchope, ed., *They Found Buried Cities*. Chicago: University of Chicago Press, 1974.
23. Quoted in John Roach, "Photo in the News: Oldest Known Maya Mural Reveals Royal Tale," *National Geographic*, December 13, 2005. http://news.nationalgeographic.com.
24. Leonard Everett Fisher, *Gods and Goddesses of the Ancient Maya*. New York: Holiday House, 1999, p. 11.
25. Miller, *Maya Art and Architecture*, p. 162.
26. David Carrasco, *Religions of Mesoamerica*. Prospect Heights, IL: Waveland, 1990, p. 110.
27. Quoted in Meyer and Gallenkamp, *The Mystery of the Ancient Maya*, p. 96.
28. Meyer and Gallenkamp, *The Mystery of the Ancient Maya*, p. 97.
29. Berthold Riese, "The Star System," *UNESCO Courier*, November 1993, p. 22.
30. Heather McKillop, *The Ancient Maya: New Perspectives*. Santa Barbara, CA: ABC-CLIO, 2004, p. 282.
31. Sharer and Traxler, *The Ancient Maya*, p. 720.

Chapter Four: How Did Trade Help Unify Maya Society?

32. Meyer and Gallenkamp, *The Mystery of the Ancient Maya*, p. 139.
33. Foster, *Handbook to Life in the Ancient Maya World*, p. 319.

34. Sharer and Traxler, *The Ancient Maya*, p. 84.
35. Schlesinger, *Animals and Plants of the Ancient Maya*, p. 55.
36. Arthur J. Mann, "The Economic Organization of the Ancient Maya," *Americas*, vol. 30, no. 2, 1973, p. 219.
37. Meyer and Gallenkamp, *The Mystery of the Ancient Maya*, p. 85.
38. Sharer and Traxler, *The Ancient Maya*, p. 84.
39. Quoted in Sharer and Traxler, *The Ancient Maya*, p. 41.
40. Culbert, *Maya Civilization*, p. 58.

Chapter Five: How Did Environmental Issues Contribute to the Collapse of Maya Society?

41. Charles Gallenkamp, *Maya: The Riddle and Rediscovery of a Lost Civilization*. New York: David McKay, 1959, p. 154.
42. Michael D. Coe, *The Maya*. New York: Thames and Hudson, 2011, p. 169.
43. Robert J. Sharer, *The Ancient Maya*, 5th ed. Stanford, CA: Stanford University Press, 1994, p. 346.
44. Quoted in Stefan Lovgren, "Climate Change Killed Off Maya Civilization, Study Says," *National Geographic*, March 13, 2003. http://news.nationalgeographic.com.
45. Quoted in Dauna Coulter, "The Fall of the Maya: 'They Did It to Themselves,'" NASA Science, October 6, 2009. https://science.nasa.gov.
46. Sharer and Traxler, *The Ancient Maya*, p. 641.
47. Sharer and Traxler, *The Ancient Maya*, p. 81.
48. Quoted in Coulter, "The Fall of the Maya."
49. Quoted in Coulter, "The Fall of the Maya."
50. Joseph Stromberg, "Why Did the Mayan Civilization Collapse?," *Smithsonian*, August 23, 2012. ww.smithsonianmag.com.

FOR FURTHER RESEARCH

Books

Charles River Editors, *A Day in the Life of the Maya*. Cambridge, MA: Charles River, 2017.

Michael D. Coe, *Breaking the Maya Code*. 3rd ed. New York: Thames and Hudson, 2012.

Michael D. Coe and Stephen D. Houston, *The Maya*. 9th ed. New York: Thames and Hudson, 2015.

Stephen Currie, *Mayan Mythology*. Farmington Hills, MI: Lucent, 2012.

Justin Jennings, *Maya: Secrets of Their Ancient World*. Gatineau, QC, Canada: Canadian Museum of History, 2013.

Victor Montejo, *Popul Vuh: A Sacred Book of the Maya*. Toronto: Groundwood, 2009.

Charles Phillips, *The Illustrated Encyclopedia of Aztec and Maya*. London: Southwater, 2017.

David Stuart, *The Maya: Voices in Stone*. New York: Turner, 2016.

INTERNET SOURCES

James Doyle, "Ancient Maya Sculpture," Metropolitan Museum of Art, 2016. www.metmuseum.org/toah/hd/mayas/hd_mayas.htm.

Metropolitan Museum of Art, "Maya Area, 500–1000 A.D." www.metmuseum.org/toah/ht/06/caa.html.

NOVA, "Expert Q&A." www.metmuseum.org/toah/ht/06/caa.html.

NOVA, "Maya." www.pbs.org/wgbh/nova/ancient/maya.html.

Smithsonian National Museum of the American Indian, "Living Maya Time," 2017. https://maya.nmai.si.edu/maya.

Erik Vance, "In Search of the Lost Empire of the Maya," *National Geographic*, September 2016. www.nationalgeographic.com/magazine/2016/09/maya-empire-snake-kings-dynasty-mesoamerica.

Stephen Currie has written many books for young adults and children. His works for ReferencePoint Press include *Women World Leaders*, *Goblins*, and *Medieval Punishment and Torture*. He has also taught grade levels ranging from kindergarten to college. He lives in New York's Hudson Valley.